# Beautiful In God's Eyes

*Understanding the Purpose and Power of Women*

Arjumand Abdullah

**Chennai • Bangalore**

CLEVER FOX PUBLISHING
Chennai, India

Published by CLEVER FOX PUBLISHING 2023
Copyright © Arjumand Abdullah 2023

All Rights Reserved.
ISBN: 978-93-56487-11-6

This book has been published with all reasonable efforts taken to make the material error-free after the consent of the author. No part of this book shall be used, reproduced in any manner whatsoever without written permission from the author, except in the case of brief quotations embodied in critical articles and reviews.

The Author of this book is solely responsible and liable for its content including but not limited to the views, representations, descriptions, statements, information, opinions and references ["Content"]. The Content of this book shall not constitute or be construed or deemed to reflect the opinion or expression of the Publisher or Editor. Neither the Publisher nor Editor endorse or approve the Content of this book or guarantee the reliability, accuracy or completeness of the Content published herein and do not make any representations or warranties of any kind, express or implied, including but not limited to the implied warranties of merchantability, fitness for a particular purpose. The Publisher and Editor shall not be liable whatsoever for any errors, omissions, whether such errors or omissions result from negligence, accident, or any other cause or claims for loss or damages of any kind, including without limitation, indirect or consequential loss or damage arising out of use, inability to use, or about the reliability, accuracy or sufficiency of the information contained in this book.

# Dedication

**In loving memory of my beloved grandfather, Ahmed Abdullah,**

You were the beacon of wisdom and the epitome of grace. Your unwavering love, boundless support, and timeless lessons have been the guiding stars on my path. This book is a tribute to your enduring legacy and the values you instilled in me. Your memory lives on in every word, and your spirit continues to inspire. Thank you for being the source of strength and the embodiment of resilience. This is for you, my dear Bapa, with profound love and gratitude.

You will remain in my heart forever,

Arjumand.

# Contents

*Foreword ......................................................................... v*
*Preface ........................................................................ vii*
*Acknowledgments ........................................................ viii*
*Introduction ................................................................... x*

**1.** Identity And Self-Discovery: Unveiling Your True Self Through Faith ............................................ 1
**2.** The Roles We Play: Embracing Adaptability ............ 7
**3.** Beliefs – Shaping Attitudes And Reactions ............ 16
**4.** Strength – Leveraging Our Advantages ................. 27
**5.** Weaknesses - Embracing Acceptance And Transformation ........................................................ 47
**6.** Independence - Balancing Autonomy And Connection ................................................................ 56
**7.** Resilience – Silent Strength ..................................... 65
**8.** Power – The Ultimate Avatar: Owning Who You Are ............................................................ 75

*Conclusion ................................................................... 83*
*About The Author ........................................................ 85*

# Foreword

It is a great honor to contribute a few words to the introduction of "Beautiful in God's Eyes – The Purpose and Power of Women," a book penned by Arjumand Abdullah. This book encapsulates an incredible journey, offering a powerful testament to the potential that lies within every woman.

Arjumand has artfully articulated her profound insights, bridging faith and empowerment, to inspire women to embrace their authentic selves. Her dedication to knowledge and understanding shines through every page, empowering readers with faith-driven principles and life-transforming advice.

In these pages, you'll discover a treasure trove of wisdom and guidance, drawn from a rich tapestry of faith, experience, and a sincere passion for empowering women. This book provides a roadmap for women seeking purpose, encouragement, and strength.

I commend Arjumand for her unwavering commitment to uplifting and supporting women on their unique journey to self-discovery and empowerment. As I read this book, I was deeply moved by the sincerity and dedication evident in every chapter. This work is not merely a collection of words; it's a heartfelt conversation, an unwavering source of guidance, and a testimony to the incredible resilience and strength of women.

May this book serve as a beacon of light for women navigating their path, guiding them to find their unique strength and purpose. I encourage you to delve into its pages, soak in the wisdom, and allow its message to inspire you.

Warm Regards,

*A.S. Fathima Muzaffar, M.C.*
**B.Com B.A. Arabic Afzalul Ulama Aalima M.A. Islamic Studies**
**Councilor,** *Egmore, Ward 61*
**National President**, *Indian Union Muslim League, Women's Wing*
**Vice President**, *All India Muslim Women Association.*

# Preface

Women of every culture and society are facing the dilemma of identity. Traditional views of what it means to be a woman and changing cultural and marital roles are causing women to conflict in their relationships with men. Women are under tremendous stress as they struggle to discover who they are and what role they are to play today—in the family, the community, and the world.

This book examines the attitude towards women and addresses vital issues such as: Are women and men equal? How is a woman unique from a man? What do the ancient scriptures really teach us about women? What is the purpose of the woman? Should women be in leadership? What are a woman's emotions and desires all about? What is a woman's potential?

To live successfully in the world, women need a new awareness of who they are and new skills to meet today's challenges. Whether you are a woman or a man, married or single, this book will help you to understand the woman as she was meant to be!

**Arjumand Abdullah**
*Date: Oct 2023*

# Acknowledgments

*I* would like to express my heartfelt gratitude to the Almighty Allah (SWT), the Most Merciful and Most Compassionate, for granting me the wisdom and inspiration to embark on this transformative journey.

I am deeply thankful to my family and friends who provided unwavering support, encouragement, and understanding throughout the writing process. Your belief in this project has been a constant source of motivation.

I extend my appreciation to the countless scholars, teachers, and mentors whose knowledge and guidance have been instrumental in shaping the content of this book. Your wisdom has been invaluable.

I would also like to acknowledge Mr. Dhananjay Modgalya for his guidance, motivation, and efforts of streamlining this process and making it doable.

Lastly, but certainly not least, I want to express my gratitude to the readers. Your interest in exploring the purpose and power of women is a testament to the importance of this topic. It is my hope that this book serves as a source of enlightenment and empowerment on your journey.

With deep appreciation,

Arjumand.

# Introduction

"Beautiful in God's Eyes: Understanding the Purpose and Power of Women" emerges as a beacon of strength and guidance for women from all walks of life. Through the lens of Islamic teachings, this enlightening journey explores the intricate tapestry of a woman's existence, revealing the profound wisdom that lies within.

With each chapter, we embark on a transformative odyssey through the facets of womanhood, from recognizing and leveraging our strengths to embracing our vulnerabilities and setting boundaries. We delve into the realms of resilience, power, and ultimately, the alignment of our life's purpose with our divine identity.

This book weaves together the timeless wisdom of our Ultimate Guidebook – The Quran. Through these timeless scriptures, women are reminded of their cherished place in the divine plan, affirming their roles as leaders, caregivers, and pillars of strength. It further illustrates the poignant stories of Muslim women who have triumphed over adversity and practical guidance to help readers uncover their inner strength. It empowers women to embrace their true selves, tap into their silent yet potent resilience, and find their authentic power. It is an invaluable companion on the path to self-discovery, offering solace and support to those navigating the intricate terrain of womanhood. Through these pages, women will be inspired to embark on a transformative journey toward embracing their authentic selves and discovering the wisdom that resides within them.

As we embark on this transformative journey, we will delve into the profound significance of women in Islam, discovering how their power transcends the boundaries of culture and circumstance. We will explore the multifaceted nature of femininity and the strength that flows from self-acceptance. Together, we will navigate the realms of resilience, independence, and authentic power, unlocking the door to a brighter, more purposeful tomorrow.

"Beautiful in God's Eyes" is an invitation to every woman to embrace her identity, find her voice, and live her purpose. It is a testament to the strength, wisdom, and boundless potential that make women not only beautiful but powerful in the eyes of God. Through these pages, may every woman discover the profound truth— that she is, indeed, a masterpiece in the divine design.

# Identity And Self-Discovery: Unveiling Your True Self Through Faith

*"Know your worth and embrace your unique identity. In the eyes of the Creator, you are a masterpiece."*

**– Unknown**

*W*elcome to a journey of self-discovery like no other. As Muslim women, we often find our strength in faith. This book, "Beautiful in God's Eyes," is your guide to understanding the power and purpose that lies within you. And it all begins with the exploration of your identity.

In this chapter, we've set the foundation for a remarkable journey of self-discovery rooted in faith. Understanding your identity is the first step toward unleashing your power and purpose as a Muslim woman. As we move forward, we'll explore deeper aspects of your identity, strengths, and the incredible potential that lies within you. Stay inspired, for the path to self-discovery is also a path to the divine within you.

Why is this journey so significant? Your identity is nothing but your compass, your map, and your mirror. It defines who you are, shapes your beliefs and actions, and guides your interactions with the world. By understanding your identity, you unlock the door to personal growth and empowerment.

## Identity - Unveiling the Divine Blueprint

In the grand tapestry of existence, one thread holds a unique and irreplaceable place—the thread of identity. It is a thread woven by the Divine Hand, a thread that runs through the very core of our being, defining who we are and why we are here. So let us embark on a journey of self-discovery and empowerment, seeking to understand the purpose and power of women, especially in the context of our faith.

Identity is a complex and multifaceted concept. It's the sum total of who we are—our beliefs, values, experiences, and the roles we occupy in this world. It's the essence of what makes us unique individuals. Yet, identity is more than just a compilation of life's experiences. It's a reflection of our deepest connection—with our Creator. Identity is not just a name or a face. It's the complex interplay of cultural, social, and personal aspects that make you unique. It's the lens through which you perceive the world and the mirror that reflects your values and beliefs.

So, the question is why is identity so important? Understanding the importance of identity is crucial, especially for women navigating a world filled with diverse expectations and roles. Our identity isn't merely a label; it's a powerful force that shapes our beliefs, actions, and the way we interact with the world. In a society often defined by norms and stereotypes, understanding our identity is our compass to navigate the path of life. Identity is vital because it influences every facet of our lives. It shapes our choices, our relationships, and even our perception of ourselves. As Muslim women, understanding our identity is essential for navigating the diverse roles and expectations we face.

## Our Identity: Rooted in Our Connection with the Creator

I believe that our identity comes from our Creator, the One who brought us into existence. He created us, not randomly, but with a divine purpose. He knows us better than anyone else ever could. He is the ultimate authority on who we truly are, and it's through our connection with Him that our true identity is unveiled. Allaah (SWT) has said in the Qur'an, "I have not created the jinns and men but to worship Me." (51:56) Our identity isn't confined to cultural norms, societal expectations, or the roles we play. It transcends all of these. Our identity is anchored in our relationship with our Creator, and it's in recognizing and nurturing this connection that we discover our true essence and purpose.

## The Fundamental Question - "Who Am I?"

The question "Who am I?" echoes through the ages, resonating deeply with our search for identity. As we delve into self-discovery, we'll peel back the layers of identity, exploring the roles we play, our personalities, our values, and our beliefs. But remember, there are no right or wrong answers. The journey of self-discovery is deeply personal and unique to you. In a world filled with external definitions, from societal expectations to media portrayal, it's crucial to take control of defining yourself. You have the power to shape your own narrative. Society may have expectations, but your personal convictions are what truly matter. By breaking free from external pressures and media-driven ideals, you can reclaim your identity on your terms.

## The Importance of Self-Discovery

So, why do we need self-discovery? Self-discovery is a transformative journey that leads to self-awareness and empowerment. It's the key to unleashing your potential. Through this process of self-discovery, you'll recognize the unique strengths, talents, and values that make you who you are. You'll uncover your purpose and passion, and gain the confidence to pursue your dreams.

## Steps to Discover Yourself

### Mindset

Cultivating a growth mindset is the first step in your journey of self-discovery. Approach this journey with curiosity, open-mindedness, and self-compassion. Understand that self-discovery is an ongoing, lifelong process. With the right mindset, you'll embrace challenges as opportunities for growth, and setbacks as stepping stones toward understanding yourself better. This mindset will empower you to face each day with a sense of wonder and purpose.

### Discovering Your True Self through Faith

Faith is a powerful lens through which you can understand your true self. Our belief systems provide profound insights into who we are. As we connect with our faith and our Creator, we open a door to self-discovery like no other.

Practical exercises, such as prayer and regular recitation of the Quran, can help you connect with your authentic self through faith. It's a journey of the heart and soul, a path to deeper self-understanding and inner peace.

As we delve deeper into the following chapters, we will explore the various facets of our identity, from embracing our strengths to understanding and overcoming our weaknesses. Together, we will navigate the intricacies of our spiritual and emotional worlds, all in the pursuit of self-discovery and empowerment as women of faith. We will uncover the rich tapestry of our identity, woven together with threads of purpose, faith, and divine love. We will understand that as Muslim women, we are indeed "Beautiful in God's Eyes," and it's through this realization that we unlock our incredible potential and power.

## *Points to Ponder and Actions to Take:*

- Define who you are: Consider journaling your thoughts and reflections to help you clarify your understanding of yourself.
- Cultivating a Growth Mindset.
- Aligning yourself with the purpose for which you were created.

# The Roles We Play: Embracing Adaptability

---

*"Adaptability is the key to survival in a changing world. Like the bamboo, we flex without breaking."*

**– Unknown**

---

*L*ife is an ever-changing play with a dynamic cast, and women often take center-stage, juggling multiple roles and responsibilities. In this chapter, we embark on a journey to explore the art of adaptability, a quintessential skill that empowers women to gracefully navigate the diverse roles they undertake.

## The Roles We Play Through Life

From the moment we take our first breath, we step onto a stage where we are daughters, sisters, wives, daughters-in-law, and mothers. These roles, though demanding, define the tapestry of our lives. Our ability to switch between these roles seamlessly is a testament to our remarkable adaptability.

As the Quran reminds us, "It is Allah who created the heavens and the earth and whatever is between them in six days; then He established Himself above the Throne." (Quran 25:59). Just as Allah created the universe, He created women with the gift of adaptability, enabling us to fulfill our roles in His divine plan.

## Why do we Adapt?

Why do women possess this extraordinary ability to adapt? It's the delicate interplay of societal expectations, personal aspirations, and cultural influences. These influences shape our journey, and by understanding them, we can better comprehend the "why" of our adaptability. This section encourages self-reflection. Why do you adapt? Is it societal pressure, personal choice, or a blend of both? Understanding our motivations is the first step toward embracing adaptability on our terms.

Adaptability is the secret strength that women inherently possess. It's about embracing change, switching hats, and adjusting to the different roles we play in our lives. From motherhood to careers, we are the ultimate shape-shifters. Real-life examples of women who've effortlessly transitioned from one role to another serve as a testament to our remarkable adaptability.

1. ***Malala Yousafzai:*** Malala is known for her extraordinary adaptability as an advocate for girls' education and women's rights. Despite facing threats and violence, she continued to speak out for the right to education. Her ability to shift from a young girl in Pakistan's Swat Valley to a global symbol of resilience and empowerment is awe-inspiring.

2. ***Dr. Ameenah Gurib-Fakim:*** A scientist, biologist, and politician, Dr. Gurib-Fakim served as the President of Mauritius. Her journey from a career in academia to becoming the first female head of state in her country is a testament to her adaptability and ability to transition between diverse roles.

3. ***Nadiya Hussain:*** Known for winning the Great British Bake Off, Nadiya has demonstrated adaptability as she transitioned from being a stay-at-home mom and amateur baker to a successful celebrity chef, author, and television presenter.

4. ***Tawakkol Karman:*** Tawakkol Karman, a Yemeni journalist and activist, became the youngest recipient of the Nobel Peace Prize for her role in the Arab Spring. Her journey from a journalist to a prominent activist advocating for women's rights and democracy in Yemen showcases her adaptability and determination.

**5. Zainab Salbi:** Zainab Salbi, an Iraqi-American author, women's rights activist, and humanitarian, transitioned from her role as a successful businesswoman to founding Women for Women International, an organization that aids women survivors of war. Her adaptability in shifting her focus towards helping marginalized women worldwide is inspiring.

These women have demonstrated remarkable adaptability, transitioning from one role to another, and serving as inspirations for others to embrace change and excel in different facets of life. Their stories reflect the inherent strength of women to evolve and adapt.

As the Quran says, "And whoever is conscious of Allah, He will make for them a way out." (Quran 65:2). Our faith in our ability to adapt, with God's guidance, can move mountains.

However, we must realize that adaptation doesn't equate to self-sacrifice.

## Obstacles Faced When We Adapt and the Dangers of Over Adapting

Adaptation is not without its challenges. Societal norms, gender bias, and stereotypes often cast shadows on our path. Recognizing these barriers is the first step in overcoming them. Remember the Hadith, "The strong believer is better and more beloved to Allah than the weak believer." (Hadith - Sahih Muslim), affirming our adaptability as a sign of our strength and a testament to our faith.

This section sheds light on these obstacles, offering insights and strategies to overcome them. As women, we are resilient, and together, we can break through these barriers.

As we delve deeper into adaptation, we encounter the pitfalls of over-adapting. When we lose sight of our core identity and allow over-adaptation to lead to stress, burnout, and self-neglect, we must pause and reflect. We must confront the emotional and psychological toll of adapting to various roles. While adaptability is a remarkable skill, overindulgence can lead to long-term consequences. Identity crises and health issues can surface when we lose sight of our core selves. Striking a balance is crucial, and this section equips you with practical tips to set boundaries and manage your roles in a harmonious manner.

## *Setting Boundaries*

It's essential for women to set boundaries, and knowing when to say no. This may come with a hint of guilt, for we've been conditioned to be ready to sacrifice. However, over time, as others adapt to these boundaries, they come to respect them. Setting boundaries is not selfish but an act of self-preservation. Just as Allah sets boundaries in the universe, we, too, must define our limits.

Overcoming obstacles to adaptation while adhering to the principles of the Quran and Sunnah involves a methodical approach. Here is a step-by-step process to navigate these challenges. These tools and techniques can be used to care for yourself and sustain a healthy equilibrium, InShaAllah.

### Step 1: Self-Reflection and Understanding

Begin by self-reflecting on your goals, roles, and the changes you wish to adapt to. Understand that adaptation is a sign of strength, as the Hadith mentions. Embrace your capacity for change as a believer.

### Step 2: Identify Obstacles

Recognize the specific obstacles you face, such as societal norms, gender bias, or stereotypes. These may manifest in various aspects of your life, including career, family, or personal development. Awareness is the first step to overcoming them.

### Step 3: Seek Guidance from the Quran and Sunnah

Turn to the Quran and Hadith for guidance. Find verses and sayings that resonate with your situation.

Seek inspiration in stories of resilience, adaptability, and strength in the lives of Prophets and righteous individuals.

### Step 4: Cultivate Patience

Practice patience, a virtue highly regarded in Islam. Remember that adapting often requires time and perseverance. Allah tells us in the Quran, "And seek help through patience and prayer..." (Quran - Surah Al-Baqarah, 2:45).

### Step 5: Foster Community and Support

Connect with like-minded individuals who can offer support and encouragement. Sisterhood is essential in Islam, and being part of a community can provide the strength to face obstacles. The Prophet Muhammad (peace be upon him) said, "The believer to the believer is like a solid building, one part strengthens the other" (Hadith - Sahih al-Bukhari).

### Step 6: Continuous Learning and Adaptation

Continuously seek knowledge and skills to facilitate adaptation. The Quran encourages seeking knowledge as a means of personal growth and resilience.

### Step 7: Dua (Supplication)

Turn to Allah through supplication. Ask for strength, guidance, and success in your adaptive journey. The Quran teaches, "And when My servants ask you concerning Me, indeed I am near. I respond to the invocation of the supplicant when he calls upon Me" (Quran - Surah Al-Baqarah, 2:186).

## Step 8: Trust in Allah's Plan

Have faith in Allah's divine plan and timing. Trust that He will guide you through challenges. As the Quran states, "But they plan, and Allah plans. And Allah is the best of planners" (Quran - Surah Al-Anfal, 8:30).

## Step 9: Perseverance and Consistency

Stay persistent and consistent in your efforts to overcome obstacles. Prophet Muhammad (peace be upon him) said, "Do not be people without minds of your own, saying that if others treat you well you will treat them well, and that if they do wrong you will do wrong. But (instead) accustom yourselves to do good if people do good and not to do wrong if they do evil" (Hadith - Sunan Abi Dawood).

By following these steps, grounded in the principles of the Quran and Sunnah, you can navigate the challenges of adaptation with resilience, faith, and strength. Remember that, as a community of believers, together we can break through these barriers and grow stronger in the process, Bi'idhnillah.

In the grand theatre of life, women continue to astound with their adaptability. This chapter has unfurled the pages of adaptability, demonstrating the essence of our strength. As we reflect on our own roles, let us embrace our dynamic selves. The subsequent chapters will delve deeper into the essence of our power and purpose, unveiling the true beauty of being a woman. As we ponder the vast spectrum of our roles and responsibilities, we celebrate our adaptability. We embrace the change and adapt because it's ingrained in our very beings.

### *Points to Ponder and Actions to Take:*

- The WHY of adapting.
- The boundaries you need to set for yourself.
- Ways to implement the Step-by-Step process to tackle the challenges of Over-Adapting.

# Beliefs – Shaping Attitudes And Reactions

*"Our beliefs shape our reality. Believe in your strength, and you'll react with resilience."*
— **Unknown**

Our beliefs are the invisible architects of our attitudes and reactions. In this chapter, we will embark on a journey to explore the profound connection between beliefs, attitudes, and reactions. What are beliefs, and how do they form the foundation of our values and attitudes? How do these attitudes, in turn, guide our reactions to the world around us? And, more importantly, how can we recondition our beliefs for personal growth and self-empowerment?

## What Truly Shapes Our Behaviors?

At the core of our attitudes and reactions lies our beliefs. These beliefs are influenced by a multitude of factors, including past experiences, upbringing, and cultural norms. Just as a sturdy tree finds its roots in the soil, our behaviors find their roots in our beliefs. And like a tree, we can nurture new growth by altering the soil. The Quran reminds us that "Allah does not burden a soul beyond that it can bear."

(Quran 2:286) – this means we can transform our behaviors by changing our beliefs.

Our responses often seem automatic, almost like a reflex. But when we delve deeper, we realize that they are intricately tied to our emotions, triggers, and past traumas. Unpacking these complex mechanisms allows us to take control of our responses. In the Quran, it is written, "Allah intends for you ease and does not intend for you hardship." (Quran 2:185) – this ease applies to understanding and transforming our responses.

## The Link Between Beliefs, Attitudes, and Reactions

Beliefs, when firmly held, evolve into values—long-lasting standards that guide a person's life and decision-making. These values are the foundation of one's attitudes, defining how one perceives others and reacts to the circumstances they encounter.

Ultimately, attitudes determine behavior, making beliefs the driving force behind our actions. Categorizing beliefs into different types of values, such as those related to happiness, wealth, career, success, or family, allows individuals to make rational, responsible, and consistent decisions.

In addition, beliefs are also ideas that individuals hold as truths. They can be grounded in certainties such as mathematical principles, rooted in probabilities, or deeply embedded in matters of faith. Beliefs find their sources in personal experiences, cultural norms, societal expectations, and the influence of others. When a potential belief aligns with a person's inner truth and becomes part of their belief system, it shapes their attitudes and reactions.

Attitudes are the mental dispositions that shape how people interact with others and respond to their current situations. These attitudes are strongly influenced by our underlying values and beliefs. However, external factors can also impact attitudes, such as the desire to conform, peer pressure, and psychological stress. Recognizing the role of emotions and past traumas in shaping attitudes is crucial for understanding why we respond the way we do.

However, reactions are learned responses to specific situations. They are, essentially, acquired behaviors formed in response to distinct circumstances and stimuli. They result from our past experiences, beliefs, and social conditioning, shaping the way we respond to life's challenges and opportunities. Understanding the roots of these reactions is pivotal in promoting personal growth and fostering emotional intelligence. Just as our conditioning teaches us to swat a mosquito when it bites, we can condition ourselves to change our responses. Understanding our deep-rooted beliefs and preconceived notions that lead to our reactions empowers us to break free from habitual patterns.

Reconditioning is a powerful tool for personal growth, enabling us to consciously alter our beliefs and behaviors.

## Our Conditioning Behind the Way We Respond

Our upbringing and societal norms act as the architects of our conditioning. Childhood experiences etch beliefs into our minds, which subsequently influence our reactions. Gender expectations, in particular, play a pivotal role in shaping women's behavior and self-perception. But just as a bird breaks free from the eggshell, we too can break free from these constraints.

## The Ways in Which We Can Recondition Ourselves

Reconditioning is a powerful tool for personal growth. It means rewriting the script that dictates our beliefs and behaviors. The process begins with self-awareness, the key to empowerment. We must consciously change our beliefs and behaviors by acknowledging the power within us to do so.

## A Step-by-Step Process to Recondition Our Upbringing

This section offers a step-by-step guide to identifying and reevaluating beliefs rooted in our upbringing. It includes exercises to question and challenge traditional beliefs and stereotypes, empowering individuals to set new standards for themselves. It also emphasizes the importance of open conversations with family and society as we pursue personal growth.

Reevaluating and reconditioning beliefs in alignment with the Quran and Sunnah is a profound process. Here are various techniques to help challenge traditional beliefs and set new standards:

1. ***Self-Reflection (Mahasabah):*** Start by regularly reflecting on your beliefs and how they originated. Ask yourself why you hold certain beliefs and whether they align with Islamic values. Muhasabah, or self-accountability, is a fundamental aspect of personal growth in Islam.

2. ***Questioning Assumptions:*** Use critical thinking to question the beliefs you've inherited. Challenge the assumptions behind these beliefs and seek a deeper understanding. Encourage yourself to ask, "Is this belief grounded in Islamic teachings?" This helps you identify areas that need re-evaluation.

3. ***Studying Quran and Hadith:*** Dive into the Quran and Hadith to gain a deeper understanding of Islamic principles and teachings. This will serve as a solid foundation for evaluating and reconditioning your beliefs. Compare your beliefs with what the Quran and Hadith say.

4. ***Seeking Guidance (Istikhara):*** When you encounter a belief that needs re-evaluation, turn to Istikhara, a prayer for guidance. Seek Allah's guidance in understanding whether the belief aligns with His will and wisdom.

5. ***Consultation (Shura):*** Engage in open conversations with knowledgeable and wise individuals who can provide guidance on Islamic beliefs. Seek their insights on how to reconcile inherited beliefs with Islamic values.

6. ***Islamic Literature and Resources:*** Read books, articles, and listen to lectures from reputable Islamic scholars and experts. These resources can offer diverse perspectives and help you make informed decisions about your beliefs.

7. ***Family Dialogues:*** Initiate open and respectful conversations with your family members about the beliefs that need re-evaluation. Share your insights, and encourage them to participate in the process of aligning family beliefs with Islamic values.

8. ***Setting New Standards:*** Define new standards for yourself based on your re-evaluated beliefs and Islamic teachings. These standards should guide your actions and decisions in daily life.

9. ***Positive Affirmations:*** Use positive affirmations based on Islamic values. For instance, affirmations like "I am guided by the teachings of the Quran" or "I seek to live in accordance with the Sunnah of the Prophet" can reinforce your new beliefs.

10. ***Seeking Repentance (Tawbah):*** If you identify beliefs that contradict Islamic teachings, seek repentance and forgiveness from Allah. Make a sincere commitment to align your beliefs with His guidance.

11. ***Community and Support:*** Surround yourself with a supportive community of like-minded individuals who are also on a path of reevaluating and reconditioning their beliefs. Sharing experiences and learning together can be empowering.

12. ***Consistency and Patience:*** The process of reevaluating beliefs can take time and effort. Be patient with yourself and stay consistent in your pursuit of personal growth through reconditioning your beliefs.

Remember that the Quran and Sunnah emphasize personal growth, self-reflection, and the importance of aligning beliefs with Islamic values. By following these techniques, you can embark on a transformative journey of reevaluating and reconditioning your beliefs while staying true to your faith and values.

## A Step-by-Step Process to Recondition Our Mind and Beliefs

Here, we explore techniques to recondition the mind and beliefs. It's about replacing limiting beliefs with empowering ones. We dive into mindfulness, positive affirmations, and self-compassion, equipping ourselves with the tools to construct a new belief system. Reconditioning the mind and beliefs in alignment with the principles of the Quran and Sunnah is a profound process that involves several techniques. Here are various approaches to help reshape your belief system:

1. ***Mindfulness (Tafakkur):*** Mindfulness is deeply rooted in Islamic tradition. Engage in regular self-reflection and contemplation (Tafakkur) on the signs of Allah in the world around you. This practice helps you develop a profound awareness of your thoughts and beliefs. Spend time pondering over the Quranic verses and Hadith to gain deeper insights.

2. **Positive Affirmations:** Use positive affirmations that resonate with Islamic teachings. For instance, affirmations based on the 99 names of Allah or Quranic verses can be powerful tools. Repeatedly affirm statements such as "I am resilient through Allah's guidance," "I trust Allah's plan for me," or "I am worthy of His mercy." These affirmations can gradually reshape your beliefs.

3. **Self-Compassion:** Self-compassion aligns with the teachings of mercy and forgiveness in Islam. Treat yourself with the same compassion and kindness that you would offer to others. Remember that Allah is the Most Merciful and Most Forgiving, and as His creation, you deserve His love and compassion.

4. **Du'a (Supplication):** Turn to du'a to seek guidance and transformation. Ask Allah to help you replace limiting beliefs with empowering ones. The Quran tells us, "And when My servants ask you concerning Me, indeed I am near. I respond to the invocation of the supplicant when he calls upon Me" (Quran - Surah Al-Baqarah, 2:186).

5. **Positive Self-Visualization:** Envision your best self, based on Islamic values. Visualize yourself embodying virtues such as patience, gratitude, and resilience. The mind can be trained to believe in your potential through consistent positive visualization.

6. ***Continual Learning:*** The Quran encourages seeking knowledge. Increase your understanding of Islamic principles and teachings. The more you learn, the stronger your foundation for positive beliefs becomes.

7. ***Surrounding Yourself with Positivity:*** Associate with people who uplift and inspire you in your faith. Positive company can reinforce your beliefs and help you discard negative ones.

8. ***Dhikr (Remembrance):*** Regularly engage in Dhikr, or the remembrance of Allah. This not only fosters a closer connection with Allah but also calms the mind and encourages positive beliefs.

9. ***Islamic Literature and Resources:*** Seek out Islamic literature that offers insights into resilience, strength, and self-compassion. Reading books, articles, and listening to lectures will promote positive beliefs and a stronger connection to Islam.

10. ***Mentorship:*** Connect with a knowledgeable and spiritually grounded mentor who can guide you in aligning your beliefs with Islamic values.

By consistently applying these techniques in your life and integrating them into your daily routine, you can recondition your mind and beliefs according to the Quran and Sunnah. This process requires patience and persistence, but it can lead to a more empowered and resilient belief system. Remember that, in Islam, transformation and personal growth are highly valued, and Allah is the Most Merciful, Most Compassionate, and Most Forgiving, offering His guidance and support throughout your journey.

Beliefs shape attitudes, and attitudes shape reactions. By understanding this interconnection and embracing the concept of reconditioning, we empower ourselves to transform our responses to the world. As we continue to unravel the layers of our power and purpose, we set our sights on the next chapter, which will unveil practical tools and resources for personal transformation. Remember the words of the Quran: "Allah does not change a people's lot unless they change what is in their hearts" (Quran 13:11). Change begins within.

## *Points to Ponder and Actions to Take:*

- Make a list of your own personal beliefs that govern your attitudes and reactions.
- Classify them based on where they stem from e.g., Upbringing, myths, assumptions, etc.
- Apply ANY 3 tools (at least) mentioned in this Chapter to recondition your beliefs.

# Strength – Leveraging Our Advantages

> *"Allah does not burden a soul beyond that it can bear."*
>
> — **(Quran 2:286)**

*B*efore we delve into the empowering world of strength, it's essential to address what strength truly means. When we discuss strength, are we merely referring to physical prowess, or is it a multi-faceted concept encompassing emotional, mental, and psychological aspects? Indeed, women may not be the stronger gender in terms of physical might when compared to men, but let's embark on a thought-provoking journey to explore the very essence of strength, as we bridge the principles of faith and empowerment.

In this journey of self-discovery and empowerment, understanding and harnessing our strengths is a vital component. Strength, in its myriad forms, has the power to shape our lives and lead us toward fulfilling our ultimate purpose. This chapter delves into the multifaceted nature of strength and its profound impact on various aspects of our existence, resonating with the teachings of the Quran and the wisdom of the Sunnah.

## *What is Strength and How Do We Define Strength?*

Strength is not a unidimensional concept, rather, it encompasses mental fortitude, emotional resilience, and physical vitality. To better appreciate the role of strength in our lives, we must examine the evolving perceptions of strength within our cultures and societies. Strength goes beyond the mere physical, and it is essential for readers to embark on a personal journey to define what strength means to them, taking inspiration from verses in the Quran that highlight the power of strength and perseverance. I believe strength transcends the boundaries of the physical realm. It extends to the emotional, mental, and psychological domains, shaping our identity as women.

So, let us tackle the ultimate question, are men and women equal? In the realm of faith, the notion of equality between men and women is distinct from the secular perspective. It doesn't involve competing to be the same, as Islam assigns unique roles and duties to each gender. Equality, according to Islamic principles, is rooted in divine recognition of these roles. Understanding our inherent strengths and re-evaluating our self-value is the path to true empowerment. Therefore, we, as women, are not in competition with men. Islam acknowledges the roles assigned to each gender by the Creator, recognizing that equality lies in the eyes of the Divine. We, therefore must reflect on our innate strengths and redefine our self-worth, and not be influenced by the concept of Gender Equality propagated by the Feminist Movement.

## Our Emotions - Our Strength or Weakness?

Emotions play a significant role in defining our strength and resilience. They are often misconstrued as weaknesses. From the Islamic perspective, emotional intelligence and resilience are celebrated as virtues. Islam recognizes the importance of emotional intelligence and encourages us to harness our emotional capacities as strengths. This section delves into the ways in which we can transform emotional vulnerabilities into sources of inner power, drawing wisdom from Islamic teachings that emphasize the importance of patience and gratitude as tools to build emotional strength.

The Quran and Sunnah teach us the importance of patience and gratitude, which can transform emotional vulnerabilities into wellsprings of inner power. Let's harness our emotions to fortify our spirits and achieve our purpose.

Transforming emotional vulnerabilities into sources of inner power is a process rooted in Islamic teachings that emphasize patience and gratitude.

Here's a step-by-step method to help you achieve this transformation:

1. ***Self-awareness:*** Begin by identifying your emotional vulnerabilities. Reflect on the emotions and situations that trigger your vulnerabilities. This self-awareness is crucial for initiating change.

2. ***Understand the Purpose of Emotions:*** Recognize that emotions are a natural part of being human. In Islam, emotions are not inherently negative; they serve a purpose. For example, sadness can lead to reflection, anger can fuel positive change, and fear can lead to caution.

3. ***Patience (Sabr):*** Embrace the concept of Sabr, or patience, as taught in the Quran and Hadith. Understand that Sabr is not passive endurance but active perseverance. It involves enduring difficulties while maintaining faith, gratitude, and hope in Allah's wisdom. Use Sabr as a tool to face your vulnerabilities without despair.

4. ***Gratitude (Shukr):*** Practice Shukr, or gratitude, as a means to shift your focus from vulnerabilities to blessings. Regularly engage in gratitude exercises

where you acknowledge and appreciate the positive aspects of your life. Gratitude helps reframe your perspective.

5. ***Seek Support:*** Share your vulnerabilities with a trusted friend, family member, or a therapist. Seeking support is an essential step in the transformation process. In the Quran, Allah encourages believers to help one another.

6. ***Positive Affirmations:*** Use positive affirmations rooted in Islamic teachings to reinforce your emotional strength. For example, repeat affirmations such as "I trust Allah's plan for me," "I am resilient through Allah's guidance," or "Every trial has a purpose in my growth."

7. ***Du'a (Supplication):*** Turn to Allah in prayer and supplication. Ask for strength and guidance to overcome emotional vulnerabilities. Du'a is a powerful tool for seeking help from the Most Merciful.

8. ***Self-Compassion:*** Be gentle with yourself. Recognize that everyone experiences vulnerabilities, and they do not diminish your worth. Practice self-compassion, as it aligns with the concept of Allah's mercy and compassion.

9. ***Analyze Triggers:*** Analyze the situations or triggers that exacerbate your vulnerabilities. Is there a recurring pattern? Identifying these triggers allows you to develop strategies for managing them.

10. ***Develop Coping Strategies:*** With the help of Sabr and Shukr, develop healthy coping strategies. Engage in activities that nurture emotional well-being, such as prayer, meditation, exercise, or spending time with loved ones.

11. ***Journaling:*** Keep a journal to document your emotional vulnerabilities, your progress in handling them, and moments of strength. Journaling serves as a reflective tool to track your growth.

12. ***Set Goals:*** Set achievable goals for yourself. Progress may be gradual, so establish milestones to celebrate your emotional strength and transformation along the way.

13. ***Consistency:*** Understand that the process of transforming vulnerabilities into inner power requires consistent effort. Be patient and persistent in your journey.

14. ***Seek Islamic Guidance:*** Consult Islamic scholars or spiritual leaders for guidance in navigating emotional vulnerabilities within the framework of Islamic teachings.

Remember that Allah is the Turner of hearts and the Source of inner strength. Through patience, gratitude, and faith, you can transform emotional vulnerabilities into sources of inner power, aligning your emotional well-being with the teachings of Islam. This transformation is not only a journey of self-discovery but also a means to strengthen your connection with the Divine.

## *Leveraging Our Mental Strength*

Mental strength is the bedrock upon which we build our resilience, overcome challenges, and achieve our aspirations. It encompasses the unwavering determination and resilience to weather life's storms. Islamic teachings emphasize steadfastness and trust in Allah's plan, equipping us with tools to develop our mental fortitude. In addition, cultivating our mental strength is a cornerstone for staying resolute in our faith.

In this section, we will explore the significance of mental strength and its pivotal role in personal development. We will identify areas for mental strength improvement, such as resilience and determination while incorporating guidance from the Quran and Hadith, which underline the value of steadfastness in the face of adversity. We will further delve into practical steps for enhancing our mental strength, aligning our pursuits with faith-inspired principles.

Enhancing mental strength in alignment with faith-inspired principles is a transformative journey. Here's a step-by-step method to help you enhance your mental strength:

1. *Self-awareness:* Begin by understanding your current mental state. Reflect on your thoughts, emotions, and areas where you feel mentally challenged. Self-awareness is the first step in transformation.

2. *Turn to Faith:* Recognize that mental strength is deeply intertwined with your faith. Faith provides a strong foundation to build mental resilience. Strengthen your connection with Allah through regular prayer, supplication, and Quranic recitation.

3. *Positive Affirmations:* Embrace positive affirmations rooted in faith. Create a list of affirmations that resonate with your beliefs. For example, affirmations like "I trust Allah's plan for me," "My faith is my source of strength," or "I can overcome challenges with Allah's guidance."

4. *Gratitude Practice:* Engage in daily gratitude exercises. Reflect on your blessings, no matter how small they may seem. Gratitude shifts your focus from what's lacking to what you already have, promoting mental strength.

5. ***Mindful Meditation:*** Incorporate mindfulness meditation into your routine. Mindful breathing and reflection are valuable tools for calming the mind and increasing mental clarity. It aligns with the Islamic concept of reflection (Tadabbur).

6. ***Seek Knowledge:*** Knowledge empowers the mind. Dedicate time to learning more about your faith through Quranic studies, Hadith, and the teachings of scholars. Seek knowledge to strengthen your belief system.

7. ***Tawakkul (Reliance on Allah):*** Develop trust in Allah's plan. Understand that your efforts, combined with trust in Allah's wisdom, lead to mental strength. Practice Tawakkul by putting in your best effort and then placing your trust in Allah.

8. ***Du'a (Supplication):*** Turn to Allah in prayer and supplication. Ask for mental strength, clarity, and resilience. Du'a is a powerful tool for seeking help from the Most Merciful.

9. ***Self-Reflection:*** Regularly engage in self-reflection. Assess your thoughts and emotions, and identify areas where you need improvement. Self-reflection leads to personal growth.

10. ***Embrace Challenges:*** Embrace challenges as opportunities for growth. Understand that adversity is a natural part of life. Approach challenges with faith and resilience, viewing them as a means of becoming mentally stronger.

11. ***Community Support:*** Connect with like-minded individuals who share your faith values. A supportive community can provide encouragement and a sense of belonging, which contributes to mental strength.

12. ***Personal Values:*** Define your core values. Your values should align with your faith and guide your decision-making process. When your actions reflect your values, mental strength is reinforced.

13. ***Professional Help:*** If you're facing severe mental health challenges, don't hesitate to seek professional help. Consulting a therapist or counselor can be an essential part of enhancing mental strength.

14. ***Consistency:*** Mental strength is a skill that requires consistent practice. Be patient with yourself and practice regular mental strength exercises.

15. ***Celebrate Progress:*** Acknowledge your progress along the way. Celebrate moments of mental clarity, resilience, and personal growth as signs of enhanced mental strength.

16. ***Charity and Acts of Kindness:*** Engage in acts of charity and kindness. These actions not only benefit others but also promote feelings of fulfillment and mental well-being.

Enhancing mental strength is an ongoing process. By combining faith-inspired principles with practical exercises, you'll find yourself better equipped to face life's challenges and remain mentally resilient. Remember that your connection with Allah is a constant source of mental strength and guidance.

## *Harnessing Physical Strength*

While women may have unique physical strengths, these should not be underestimated. Our physical well-being is an integral part of our empowerment journey. The Quran and Hadith remind us of the importance of maintaining good health, making it an act of worship. We will explore ways to nurture our physical strengths through exercise, nutrition, and self-care, ensuring that our bodies are strong and ready for life's challenges.

Women possess unique natural physical strengths, and these assets can be nurtured through mindful self-care, exercise, and a balanced approach to nutrition. It is crucial to acknowledge that physical well-being is intrinsically linked to our overall empowerment, and this section will reinforce that perspective with references to the importance of maintaining good health as described in Islamic teachings.

Empowering physical well-being through a daily practical routine is not only important but also attainable. Here's a step-by-step guide to help you embrace this journey:

1. ***Morning Intentions:*** Start your day with Fajr Salah. Try and wake up for Tahajjud. In the quiet moments of the morning, set your focus on maintaining good physical health as an act of worship and self-care, aligning it with your faith. There is a hadith (saying of the Prophet Muhammad, peace be upon him) that highlights the blessings (barakah) in the morning time. It is narrated in Sahih Muslim:

    The Prophet Muhammad (peace be upon him) said: "In the morning, charity is due on every joint of every one of you. Every utterance of Allah's glorification is an act of charity, every utterance of His greatness is an act of charity, every utterance of His power is an act of charity, every utterance of His sovereignty is an act of charity, and every utterance of His praise is an act of charity, every utterance of His greatness is an act of charity, and every utterance of His power is an act of charity, and every utterance of His goodness is an act of charity, and every act of charity is an act of charity, and every act of his goodness is an act of charity." (Sahih Muslim)

This hadith emphasizes that every moment in the morning is a time for blessings and acts of charity, whether through words of praise and glorification of Allah or through physical acts of charity. It encourages believers to start their day with gratitude and acts of worship.

2. ***Hydration Ritual:*** Begin your day by drinking a glass of water. Proper hydration is the cornerstone of physical well-being. Make it a habit to drink water at regular intervals during the day. Staying hydrated is a practice that not only benefits your physical well-being but is also in line with the teachings of moderation in Islam.

3. ***Mindful Movement:*** Incorporate mindful movement into your morning routine. Engage in activities like yoga, stretching, or light exercises to awaken your body and mind. It is a Sunnah of a beloved Prophet Muhammed (SAW) to go for a walk. Physical activity is not only beneficial for your health but also a way to express gratitude for the body that Allah has blessed you with. Performing Salat ul Duha is the best way to express gratitude to Allah SWT for the physical body. By combining Salat ad-Duha with the practice of gratitude for your body and overall well-being, you can establish a deeper connection with your Creator and recognize

the importance of maintaining and cherishing the physical health that Allah has provided.

4. ***Nutrient-Rich Breakfast:*** Consume a nutritious breakfast that includes a balance of protein, healthy fats, and carbohydrates. Refer to Islamic dietary guidelines and Sunnah foods for inspiration. Incorporate foods such as dates, olives, and honey, which have been praised for their health benefits in Islamic traditions.

5. ***Hygiene and Self-Care:*** Follow Islamic practices of cleanliness and personal hygiene. Perform Wudu (ablution) as a spiritual and physical cleansing ritual, which also ensures good hygiene.

6. ***Sunnah Foods:*** Explore incorporating Sunnah foods such as black seeds, honey, and figs into your daily diet. These have been highly regarded for their health benefits in Islamic traditions.

7. ***Prayer and Movement:*** Integrate short movements into your daily routine, even while at work or home. Consider stretching during your breaks or incorporating quick prayer movements. These activities keep you physically active throughout the day.

8. ***Balance in Nutrition:*** Follow a balanced diet based on Islamic dietary principles. Avoid overindulgence and follow the guidelines of eating in moderation. Remember that your body is an Amanah (trust) from Allah.

9. ***Movement Breaks:*** Incorporate short movement breaks throughout your day. Stand up, stretch, and take a quick walk. These practices are consistent with Sunnah and help maintain good physical health.

10. ***Daily Self-Care:*** Dedicate time each day for self-care practices. It could be as simple as moisturizing your skin, brushing your hair, or massaging your hands and feet with natural oils. This self-care routine helps you appreciate and care for the physical vessel entrusted to you by Allah.

11. ***Evening Reflection:*** In the evening, reflect on your daily self-care and physical well-being practices. Express gratitude for the health you have and recite the evening Adhkaar.

12. ***Quality Sleep:*** Prioritize sleep and create a bedtime routine that allows for restful sleep. Islam encourages a balanced approach to rest and wakefulness, underscoring the importance of adequate sleep.

13. **Consistency:** Consistency is the key. Make these practices a part of your daily routine, just as you do with your five daily prayers. By consistently nurturing your physical well-being, you're acknowledging the importance of taking care of the body that Allah has blessed you with.

14. **Consultation:** If you have specific health concerns or questions, don't hesitate to consult with healthcare professionals or experts. Seeking advice and guidance aligns with Islamic principles that emphasize the importance of preserving one's health.

Embracing a daily practical routine that promotes physical well-being can be an act of worship and a means to strengthen your empowerment. It's about nurturing the unique strengths Allah has bestowed upon women, caring for your body as an Amanah, and being the best version of yourself in service to Allah and those around you.

## *Leveraging Our Strengths for Success*

The true measure of strength is in its application. We will explore how to channel our strengths to achieve success in our daily lives, careers, relationships, and personal growth. By embracing our unique capabilities, we not only uplift ourselves but also those around us. Strength, when wielded effectively, can serve as a catalyst for personal and collective advancement. Success stories and examples of women who have harnessed their strengths will serve as inspirations for our own journeys. Here are a few inspirational success stories and examples of women who have harnessed their strengths, we gain insights into how their unique capabilities can propel them to excellence.

During the time of Prophet Muhammad (peace be upon him), many remarkable women demonstrated their strengths and harnessed their unique capabilities in various aspects of life. Their stories continue to inspire women today:

1. ***Khadijah bint Khuwaylid (may Allah be pleased with her):*** Khadijah, the first wife of the Prophet Muhammad, was a successful businesswoman. She possessed immense strength in her ability to manage her trade, which eventually led to her employing the Prophet Muhammad (PBUH). Her steadfast support, unwavering belief, and the financial stability she provided allowed the Prophet to focus on his mission.

2. ***Aisha bint Abi Bakr (may Allah be pleased with her):*** Aisha (RA) was known for her exceptional memory and deep knowledge of Islamic teachings. Her strength lay in her scholarship and her willingness to share her knowledge with the entire community. She was a respected teacher, and her narrations of Hadith continue to be a source of guidance for Muslims.

3. ***Fatimah bint Muhammad (may Allah be pleased with her):*** Fatimah (RA), the daughter of the Prophet Muhammad, exemplified strength in her resilience and commitment to her faith. She faced numerous challenges in her life, including the loss of her mother and the difficult circumstances of early Islam. Her strength was her unwavering devotion to Allah and her family.

4. ***Umm Waraqah (may Allah be pleased with her):*** Umm Waraqah was one of the early converts to Islam. She is known for her dedication to the Quran and her role as a scribe. Her strength was in preserving the Quranic revelations in writing, ensuring that the message of Islam was documented accurately.

5. ***Nusaybah bint Ka'ab (may Allah be pleased with her):*** Nusaybah, also known as Umm Ammarah, was a strong and courageous woman on the battlefield. She participated in battles alongside the Prophet Muhammad, demonstrating physical strength and unwavering commitment to the cause of Islam.

6. ***Umm Sulaym (may Allah be pleased with her):*** Umm Sulaym was a woman of profound strength in her character and resilience. She was known for her kindness, charity, and wisdom. Her strength was in her ability to provide emotional support and guidance to her family and the community.

7. ***Asma bint Abi Bakr (may Allah be pleased with her):*** Asma, the daughter of Abu Bakr, demonstrated immense physical strength and resilience during the migration from Makkah to Madinah. She played a crucial role in providing provisions and support to her family during this challenging journey.

8. ***Sumayyah bint Khayyat (may Allah be pleased with her):*** Sumayyah is renowned as the first martyr in Islam. She displayed immense strength by refusing to renounce her faith under torture and persecution. Her unwavering belief and steadfastness serve as an enduring example of spiritual strength.

These women from the time of Prophet Muhammad (PBUH) exhibited a diverse range of strengths, from business acumen and knowledge to courage and resilience. Their examples emphasize the multifaceted nature of women's strength and how it can be harnessed for personal growth, community advancement, and the pursuit of excellence. Their stories are a testament to the strength and capabilities inherent in women, which continue to inspire and guide women in their daily lives today.

In conclusion, this chapter underscores the importance of recognizing and using our strengths as a means of empowerment. It encourages women to embrace their multifaceted strengths, aligning their endeavors with

Islamic principles. Strength knows no gender boundaries. It's a tapestry woven with threads of resilience, determination, emotional intelligence, and physical vitality. As I wrap up this chapter, I encourage every woman to recognize and harness her strengths as a source of empowerment.

This, my dear sisters, is the essence of our feminine power. Stay tuned for the following chapter, which delves into the profound role of resilience and determination on our path to fulfilling our purpose.

## *Points to Ponder and Actions to Take:*

- Choose and implement any 3 habits you will inculcate to develop emotional resilience.
- Choose and implement any 3 habits you will inculcate to develop mental resilience.
- Choose and implement any 3 self-care routines you will inculcate to develop physical resilience.

# Weaknesses - Embracing Acceptance And Transformation

*"Weaknesses are opportunities for growth. Accept them, transform them, and watch them become your strengths."*

**– Unknown**

*I*n this chapter, we face the undeniable reality of human weaknesses and their profound impact on our lives. Firstly, by acknowledging the undeniable truth that all of us have our weaknesses. Secondly, by realizing that none of us are perfect and that the concept of perfection itself is a fallacy. We weren't created to be perfect; we were created with flaws, imperfections, and weaknesses so that we could recognize them, accept them, and choose how to navigate them.

Thus, as we embark on a transformative journey, we'll explore the relationship between our weaknesses, self-identity, and empowerment, discovering that the path to strength often begins with acceptance.

## *Embracing Our Imperfections*

We start by emphasizing the vital first step: acceptance. It's essential to acknowledge our weaknesses, to be free from the misconception that we have none. Every human has their weaknesses, and the key to transformation lies in acceptance. As we explore the question of whether it's inherently bad to have weaknesses, we discover that it's actually not. In fact, it's our weaknesses that make us human. In our moments of vulnerability, it is our inherent weakness that drives us to seek strength from our Creator. The Quran reminds us of the power of patience and prayer, stating, "Seek help through patience and prayer" (Quran, 2:45). Patience is the unwavering resolve to endure trials with fortitude, while prayer connects us to the divine source of all strength. Together, they provide the foundation for transforming our limitations and weaknesses into sources of resilience and inner power. In embracing our weaknesses and turning to Allah, we unlock the potential to emerge from adversity stronger, more steadfast, and spiritually fortified.

## Turning Weaknesses into Strengths

As we debunk the myth that weaknesses are insurmountable obstacles, we uncover the concept of "strength in vulnerability." By sharing stories of individuals who have turned their weaknesses into strengths, we learn that our vulnerabilities can serve as stepping stones to greatness.

One of the most powerful examples of turning weakness into strength can be found in the story of the Prophet Moses (Musa, peace be upon him). Despite being chosen as a prophet and messenger by Allah, Moses initially struggled with his speech impediment. This vulnerability made him feel inadequate when he was tasked with confronting Pharaoh, a powerful and oppressive ruler. However, instead of succumbing to his weakness, Moses turned to Allah, seeking His guidance and support.

In Surah Taha (Quran, 20:25-28), we find this beautiful dialogue between Moses and Allah:

*"He (Musa AS) said, 'My Lord, expand for me my breast [with assurance],*

*And ease for me my task,*

*And untie the knot from my tongue,*

*That they may understand my speech.'"*

Allah granted Moses' request, enabling him to speak clearly and effectively. This story highlights how Moses transformed his speech impediment, initially seen as a weakness, into a strength. His unwavering faith in Allah, his determination, and his willingness to confront his vulnerability made him one of the most revered and powerful prophets in Islamic tradition.

This narrative demonstrates that our vulnerabilities can indeed be stepping stones to greatness when we turn to Allah and use them as opportunities for growth, learning, and self-improvement.

This episode challenges us to question whether our emotions and weaknesses are a burden or an opportunity. It all depends on how we choose to perceive and handle them. We have the power of choice. We learn that the first step is acceptance, followed by addressing our weaknesses. Ultimately, we decide whether to master these weaknesses or overcome them and turn to our Creator for help with the same.

## Converting Our Weaknesses into Strengths

This section is dedicated to practical strategies for turning weaknesses into strengths, drawing inspiration from the teachings of the Quran and Sunnah. Self-improvement and continuous learning, as highlighted in Islamic principles, serve as our compass for personal growth. We delve into the importance of seeking help and support from others and learn how to cultivate a positive and empowering mindset regarding our weaknesses.

## *Overcoming Weaknesses: A Step-by-Step Process*

To tackle our weaknesses, a structured approach is provided. We learn to identify, address, and ultimately overcome personal weaknesses through exercises and self-assessment tools. Strategies for building resilience and fostering personal growth in the face of weaknesses become our guiding principles. Here are practical strategies, inspired by the Quran and Sunnah, to turn weaknesses into strengths:

1. ***Self-Improvement and Continuous Learning:*** In the Quran, Allah encourages self-improvement through the pursuit of knowledge. The Prophet Muhammad also emphasized the value of seeking knowledge. Begin by identifying the areas where you perceive weaknesses. Then, dedicate time to learn and grow in those areas. Attend classes, read books, or take online courses that are relevant to your goals. Continuous learning and self-improvement will empower you to transform your weaknesses into strengths.

2. ***Seeking Help and Support:*** The Quran and Sunnah emphasize the importance of seeking help and support when needed. The Prophet Muhammad said, "The believer to the believer is like a solid building, one

part supports the other." Reach out to friends, family, mentors, or support groups. Share your weaknesses and ask for guidance or assistance. When you accept help, you'll discover that you don't have to tackle weaknesses on your own. Together, you will be able to find effective solutions and support one another in your journeys of personal growth.

3. ***Cultivating a Positive Mindset:*** Your mindset significantly influences your ability to turn weaknesses into strengths. The Quran teaches the importance of patience, gratitude, and optimism in facing life's challenges. Engage in positive affirmations and self-reflection. Challenge negative thoughts and replace them with empowering beliefs. For example, if you struggle with public speaking, affirm that you are improving and becoming a more effective communicator. Surround yourself with positivity, and your mindset will become a powerful tool in your transformational journey. Furthermore, enrolling for Toastmasters or TedEx will provide you with the community and motivate you to become a better communicator.

4. ***Seek Inspiration from Role Models:*** The Quran and Sunnah offer numerous role models to inspire you in your quest to overcome weaknesses. Study the stories of prophets, companions, and righteous women who faced challenges and emerged stronger. Their journeys

highlight the power of faith, resilience, and personal growth. Draw motivation from their experiences and apply the lessons to your own life.

**5. *Maintain Patience and Consistency:*** The Quran describes the importance of patience during adversity. Turning weaknesses into strengths is a process that requires time and effort. Stay patient and persistent in your pursuit. Consistency is key to real transformation. The Prophet Muhammad said, "The deeds most loved by Allah are those done regularly, even if they are small." Small, consistent actions lead to significant improvements.

**6. *Utilize Du'a (Supplication):*** Turn to Allah with your weaknesses and seek His guidance and assistance through Du'a. The Quran assures that Allah is the Bestower of strength. Pray for the strength and wisdom to overcome your weaknesses. Reflect on the times when you've overcome challenges in the past with Allah's help. This will reinforce your belief in your ability to turn your weaknesses into strengths with His support.

By implementing these strategies inspired by Islamic principles, you can embark on a journey of self-improvement, resilience, and personal growth. Remember that everyone has weaknesses, and they can serve as stepping stones to a stronger, more empowered you when approached with faith and determination.

## The Identity Question

Here, we discuss the misconception that our weaknesses define our overall worth. We explore the roles of self-acceptance and self-compassion in redefining our self-identity. Strategies for detaching from the notion that weaknesses are an intrinsic part of who we are empower us to reshape our narrative.

### Redefining Our Identity

Our weaknesses, certainly do not define our overall worth. By accepting our vulnerabilities and transforming them into strengths, we can truly redefine ourselves. We learn that true success can only be achieved when we separate weakness from identity, allowing our strengths to shine through.

The process of turning weaknesses into strengths requires a powerful mindset. This section provides insights into the importance of knowing your 'why.' Identifying the purpose behind your journey can be a transformative catalyst. Know that growth is a constant journey of learning, improving ourselves, and enhancing our skills.

An empowering mindset is the key to overcoming any weakness. This part reinforces the idea that once you identify your 'why,' your mindset shifts and there's no turning back. Your weaknesses will transform into strengths, one by one, as you become more resilient and determined in your journey.

As I conclude this chapter we are left with the wisdom that acceptance and transformation are portent tools for personal empowerment. I encourage every woman to embrace her weaknesses as the raw material for her unique strengths. We learn that acceptance is the first step and with the right mindset we can turn our vulnerabilities into strengths. In the next chapter, we will delve into the profound role of resilience and determination on our path to fulfilling our purpose illuminated by stories of remarkable Muslim women who have embodied these qualities.

### *Points to Ponder and Actions to Take:*

- List your weaknesses.
- List ways in which you can turn them into strengths.
- Take consistent action to master the weaknesses one weakness at a time. This builds tremendous confidence. Trust me!

# 6

# *Independence - Balancing Autonomy And Connection*

---

*"Independence is the ability to stand on your own, but true wisdom is knowing when to reach out and connect."*

– **Unknown**

---

*I*n this chapter, we delve into the complex concept of independence and its profound significance in the lives of women. We begin by questioning the very essence of true independence and the fervent desire for autonomy, setting the stage for a comprehensive exploration of women's pursuit of independence and the potential pitfalls associated with an obsessive quest.

We'll begin by defining what independence means and question the reality of true independence. We'll ponder the reasons behind our desire for independence and assess its value in our lives. Through stories and teachings from the Quran and Sunnah, we'll draw insights into how our faith views the concept of independence and interconnectedness.

## Defining Independence: Are We Truly Independent?

Independence is a multifaceted concept that warrants self-exploration. I challenge the idea of absolute independence and would like to shed light on the interdependence that underlies human relationships. In doing so, I recognized the multifaceted influences of society, culture, and family on a women's autonomy. This section encourages self-reflection on the complexities of independence within different life domains, ultimately leading us to question whether true independence is ever attainable.

Independence, as we define it today, is relative. While we may strive for independence, the reality is that we are fundamentally interdependent as humans. We rely on one another, and this interconnectedness is not a weakness but a divine design. In the Quran, Allah emphasizes the importance of community and supporting one another. As the Prophet Muhammad (peace be upon him) taught, "The example of believers in their affection, mercy, and compassion for each other is that of a body. When any limb aches, the whole body reacts with sleeplessness and fever." Our interconnectedness is part of our nature as human beings.

## *Do We Really Want to Be Independent?*

Let us explore the desire to be independent in-depth, with an examination of the values that underpin personal and societal motivations. I acknowledge that the pursuit of independence is a deeply personal journey that can vary from person to person. Let's explore the motivations behind the desire for independence, which can include personal growth, self-sufficiency, and autonomy. The Quran encourages self-improvement and individual striving, but it also emphasizes community and helping those in need. Independence, in the Islamic sense, is therefore, defined by our ability to fulfill our responsibilities and to contribute positively to society.

Through these thought-provoking questions, I encourage you to evaluate your own desires for independence and to contemplate what independence truly means to you as a Muslim Woman:

1. *What does independence mean to you on a personal level, and how do you define it in the context of your life?*

2. *Have you ever felt the desire for more independence in specific aspects of your life, such as your career, relationships, or personal decisions? If so, what prompted this desire?*

3. *How do societal norms and cultural expectations influence your perception of independence and autonomy as a woman?*

4. Do you believe that true independence can exist alongside interdependence and meaningful connections with others? Why or why not?

5. Reflect on a time when you felt that you lacked the independence you desired. What were the circumstances, and how did you handle this situation?

6. What are the potential benefits and drawbacks of pursuing absolute independence in various areas of your life?

7. Can you think of examples from your life or from those around you of women who have successfully balanced their desires for independence with their connections to family, friends, or their community? What can you learn from these examples?

8. What steps can you take to align your quest for independence with your personal values and faith-inspired principles while fostering meaningful relationships with others?

Reflecting on these questions can help you gain a deeper understanding of your own desires for independence and the role it plays in your life as a woman.

## The Obsession with Independence

An important facet of our exploration is the potential pitfall of an obsessive pursuit of independence. Let us scrutinize the negative consequences of neglecting vital connections and relationships in this quest for autonomy.

Moreover, let us all strive to maintain a healthy balance between independence and interdependence to ensure that we do not lose sight of the meaningful connections that bring fulfillment.

A compelling example of the perils of excessive independence and isolation can be found in the Quran's account of the Prophet Yunus (AS). When Yunus (AS), in his haste, left his people without Allah's permission, he found himself isolated within the belly of a great fish. This story serves as a profound lesson on the consequences of distancing oneself from society and the need for a balanced approach. While independence is cherished, it should not eclipse the essential connections and relationships that bring joy and fulfillment into our lives.

### Balancing Autonomy and Connection

Balancing autonomy and connection is the core of this section. We discuss the significance of finding a middle ground between independence and interdependence, exploring the importance of nurturing relationships, support networks, and a profound sense of belonging. The Quran and Sunnah stress the importance of finding a balance between autonomy and connection. We are encouraged to support one another, maintain healthy relationships, and seek help when needed. Just as we need space in our relationships, we also need personal time for self-reflection and self-improvement. Islam advocates balance in all aspects of life, and this extends to the concept of independence. Striking a balance ensures personal growth while fostering meaningful connections and a sense of belonging.

Balancing independence and interdependence from an Islamic perspective involves aligning your choices and actions with the principles of your faith. Here are practical tips for women to find this balance:

1. ***Seek Knowledge:*** Invest time in studying and understanding the teachings of the Quran and Hadith. This knowledge will guide you in making decisions that align with Islamic principles and values.
2. ***Prayer and Reflection:*** Regularly engage in prayer and reflection to seek Allah's guidance and wisdom. This spiritual practice will help you make decisions with a clear heart and mind.
3. ***Set Clear Intentions:*** Before pursuing any path, clarify your intentions. Ensure that your decisions are driven by the desire to please Allah and serve His purpose.
4. ***Consultation (Shura):*** Seek advice and consultation with knowledgeable and trustworthy individuals. Islam encourages making decisions collectively, and the wisdom of others can help you find balance.
5. ***Maintain Ties of Kinship:*** Islam places great importance on maintaining family ties. Prioritize

your relationships with family members while also seeking your independence. Strive for harmony between familial responsibilities and personal growth.

6. ***Practice Patience (Sabr):*** In times of hardship or conflicting desires, exercise patience. Trust in Allah's plan and persevere through challenges with a steadfast heart.
7. ***Gratitude (Shukr):*** Always express gratitude to Allah for the blessings you have and the support from loved ones. A grateful heart strengthens relationships and your sense of self.
8. ***Service to Others:*** Engage in community service and help those in need. Serving others nurtures both your independence and interdependence and reflects Islamic values.
9. ***Forgiveness:*** Practice forgiveness and compassion. Forgive others for their shortcomings, and forgive yourself for your imperfections. Forgiveness fosters harmonious connections.
10. ***Conflict Resolution:*** When conflicts arise in relationships, approach them with empathy, active listening, and a genuine desire for resolution, following the guidance of the Quran and Sunnah.
11. ***Open Communication:*** Maintain open and honest communication with family, friends, and your

community. Sharing your aspirations and challenges can lead to greater understanding and support.
12. ***Educate and Inspire:*** Be an example to others through your actions. Inspire your family and community by balancing your independence with strong relationships.
13. ***Regular Self-Reflection:*** Periodically assess your life and priorities. Are you maintaining the balance? Regular self-reflection helps you stay on course.

By implementing these practical tips from an Islamic perspective, you can strike a balance that allows you to grow as an individual while fostering meaningful connections with family, friends, and your community.

As I conclude this chapter, I want to leave you with a deeper understanding of your desire for independence and encourage you to reflect on your motivations. Take the time to reflect on the deeper understanding of your desire for independence and the need for a balanced approach. Independence, as seen through the lens of faith, is intertwined with our connections to our Creator and others as well. In the upcoming chapter, we will delve into the profound exploration of purpose and how it can be aligned with personal values and independence, as we continue on our journey of self-discovery and empowerment.

## Points to Ponder & Actions to Take:

- Define what independence means to you.
- Identify why it is important for you and in which area of your life.
- Find your balance.

# Resilience - Silent Strength

> *"Seek help with patience and prayer; truly it is extremely heavy and hard except for the humble-minded."*
>
> — **(Quran 2:45)**

*I*n this chapter, we delve into the profound concept of resilience as silent strength. We'll explore the role of resilience in women's lives and the importance of setting and upholding personal boundaries. Through the principles of the Quran and Sunnah, we'll understand the foundation of resilience and how to establish boundaries as a source of strength.

Resilience is the silent strength that defines whether we respond to life's challenges as victims or as optimists embracing opportunities. It is the ability to withstand adversity, losses, and adversities while seeing each failure as a chance to learn and grow. The Quran and Sunnah provide us with invaluable lessons in resilience and the importance of setting boundaries to maintain our physical, mental, and emotional health.

## How Far Can I Go?

The Quran teaches us that Allah does not burden a soul beyond that which it can bear (Quran 2:286). Resilience is an innate quality within every individual, allowing them to overcome challenges and exceed their perceived limits. By reflecting on our personal strengths and pushing our boundaries, we can harness this silent strength and realize our full potential. The story of Prophet Ibrahim's unwavering determination in the face of adversity serves as an inspirational example of resilience beyond perceived limits. Resilience empowers us to exceed our perceived limitations by pushing boundaries and recognizing the potential for growth. Just as Prophet Ibrahim displayed unwavering determination, resilience enables us to break free from self-imposed limitations and tap into our hidden strengths.

## What Can Break Me? Boundaries and Resilience

Challenges and stressors are part of life, but resilience equips us to confront them head-on. By recognizing and addressing vulnerabilities, we can build our resilience. The Quran teaches us that "With hardship comes ease" (Quran 94:6), reminding us that adversities are opportunities for personal growth. The story of Prophet Ayyub (AS) illustrates the power of resilience in the face of suffering and loss. The key is to recognize that these challenges can ultimately contribute to our personal growth.

To bolster resilience while keeping the principles of the Quran and Sunnah in mind, consider these strategies:

1. ***Tawakkul (Trust in Allah):*** Rely on Allah and trust His plan. Maintain faith that challenges are tests designed for personal growth. Recite and reflect upon verses like Surah Al-Baqarah (2:286) to strengthen your trust.

2. ***Dua (Supplication):*** Engage in sincere supplication, seeking strength and patience to endure hardships. The Prophet Muhammad (peace be upon him) said that "Dua is the essence of worship." (Tirmidhi)

3. ***Sabr (Patience):*** Practice patience and persevere through adversity. Reflect on stories of the Prophets in the Quran who endured trials with patience, such as the story of Prophets Ayub (AS) and Prophet Ibrahim (AS).

4. ***Gratitude (Shukr):*** Express gratitude for the blessings you have, even in challenging times. The Quran emphasizes that gratitude leads to an increase in blessings (Surah Ibrahim, 14:7).

5. ***Self-Reflection:*** Regularly reflect on your experiences, your reactions to challenges, and the lessons you've learned. Evaluate your growth and development.

6. ***Community Support:*** Seek support from your community, family, and friends. The sense of belonging and social support is highly encouraged in Islamic teachings.

7. ***Resilience through Adversity:*** Reflect on the stories of the Sahaba (companions) who faced incredible adversity and remained resilient. Learn from their experiences and struggles.

8. ***Self-Compassion:*** Be kind to yourself during tough times. Avoid self-criticism and practice self-compassion. The Prophet Muhammad (peace be upon him) emphasized self-compassion in his teachings.

9. ***Charity (Sadaqah):*** Engage in acts of charity and help those in need, knowing that it purifies your heart and increases your resilience. The Prophet Muhammad (peace be upon him) said, "Your smile for your brother is a charity." (Tirmidhi)

10. ***Dhikr (Remembrance of Allah):*** Engage in the remembrance of Allah through the recitation of Quranic verses and adhkaar. This practice brings inner peace and builds resilience.

11. ***Seek Knowledge:*** Pursue Islamic knowledge to understand the purpose of trials and tribulations in life. Knowledge provides clarity and helps in finding meaning in challenges.

12. ***Set Goals:*** Establish clear, achievable goals to focus on during tough times. This will give you a sense of direction and purpose.

13. ***Help Others:*** Assist those facing similar challenges. The Quran emphasizes the reward for helping others in times of difficulty.

14. ***Learn from Prophetic Teachings:*** Study the life of the Prophet Muhammad (peace be upon him) and learn from his resilience and steadfastness during trials.

15. ***Forgiveness:*** Forgive those who have wronged you, as forgiveness is a source of personal strength. Reflect on the forgiveness demonstrated by the Prophet Muhammad (peace be upon him) in his life.

16. ***Self-Care:*** Prioritize self-care, including rest, a healthy diet, exercise, and relaxation techniques. A healthy body and mind enhance resilience.

These strategies, deeply rooted in Quranic principles and Prophetic teachings, will not only help you face challenges with resilience but also turn them into opportunities for personal growth and spiritual development.

## *How Do I Set My Boundaries?*

Setting boundaries is essential for maintaining emotional and mental well-being. The Quran and Sunnah emphasize the importance of setting personal boundaries to maintain emotional and mental well-being. The Prophet Muhammad (peace be upon him) modelled good character, emphasizing the importance of respecting others and setting boundaries while demonstrating empathy and compassion. Here is some practical guidance on how to identify and communicate boundaries effectively, empowering us to protect our overall well-being.

Identifying and communicating boundaries effectively while drawing from the principles of the Quran and Sunnah is essential to protect our overall well-being. Here is some practical guidance:

1. ***Self-Reflection and Self-Knowledge:*** Begin by understanding your own limits and personal values. This self-awareness is rooted in the Islamic tradition, as we are encouraged to reflect on our actions and intentions regularly.

2. **Consult Quran and Hadith**: Turn to the Quran and Hadith for guidance. They contain principles that promote healthy boundaries, such as modesty, respect, and balance in interactions.

3. **Open and Honest Communication**: In line with the Sunnah, communicate your boundaries openly and honestly with those around you. This could include discussing your needs, expectations, and areas where you require respect or privacy.

4. **Balance and Moderation**: The Quran emphasizes the concept of balance. Apply this principle when setting boundaries to ensure they are not too rigid or too loose. Balance your rights with the rights of others.

5. **Seek Support from Scholars and Elders:** Consult with knowledgeable individuals in your community, such as scholars or elders, for guidance on setting boundaries according to Islamic principles.

6. **Stay True to Your Values:** Use your understanding of Quranic values to set boundaries that align with your faith and values. This will help you remain consistent and authentic.

7. **Respect for Others:** Remember the Islamic concept of 'Adaab' (good manners) when establishing boundaries. Show respect for others' boundaries as you expect them to respect yours.

8. **Dua (Supplication):** Pray for guidance and support in upholding your boundaries. In Islam, supplication is a powerful tool that can strengthen your resolve and protect your well-being.

9. ***Seek Guidance from Sunnah:*** The life of the Prophet Muhammad (peace be upon him) is a model for setting and maintaining boundaries. His interactions with companions and family offer valuable insights into the practice of healthy boundaries.

10. ***Consistent Self-Care:*** Use the principles of self-care from the Quran and Sunnah to protect your overall well-being. For example, ensure you take time for 'Dhikr' (remembrance of Allah), engage in acts of worship, and practice gratitude.

By following these practical steps in accordance with Quranic and Sunnah, you can effectively identify and communicate your boundaries, safeguarding your emotional, mental, and spiritual well-being.

## Can Anything Break Me?

The Quran reminds us that the human soul is resilient and capable of enduring challenges. By questioning our innate strength and recognizing the potential for resilience, we empower ourselves to face adversity with determination. The story of the Prophet Yusuf (AS) illustrates resilience in the face of betrayal, adversity, and ultimately triumph. Here are some real-life stories of Muslim women who have overcome seemingly insurmountable odds, demonstrating the incredible strength of the human spirit:

1. ***Dr. Hawa Abdi:*** A Somali gynecologist, Dr. Abdi transformed her family's farm into a refugee camp that housed thousands during Somalia's civil war. She provided medical care and shelter, even under threats from militant groups.

2. ***Zahra Lari:*** Hailing from the United Arab Emirates, Zahra Lari is known as the world's first figure-skater who competes wearing a headscarf. She overcame cultural barriers and discrimination to pursue her passion and is now an inspirational figure for Muslim athletes.

3. ***Rukhsana Kauser:*** Rukhsana, from Indian-administered Kashmir, fought off armed terrorists who attempted to kidnap her. She used her bare hands to grab one of their rifles and chased them away, saving her family.

4. ***Dilshad Ali:*** A writer and journalist, Dilshad has been a vocal advocate for the rights of disabled individuals, challenging societal norms and working to make the world more accessible for people with disabilities.

5. ***Aminah Assilmi:*** Aminah was a prominent Muslim speaker and activist. After a car accident left her in a coma and with a traumatic brain injury, she used her experience to raise awareness about disabilities within the Muslim community.

These remarkable women faced adversity, whether due to societal challenges, discrimination, or personal trauma, and emerged as beacons of hope, strength, and resilience. Their stories serve as powerful reminders of the capacity of the human spirit to triumph over adversity and inspire positive change in the world.

As I conclude this chapter, I want women to understand the depth of their silent strength and the importance of setting boundaries. Resilience, as highlighted in the Quran and Sunnah, is a testament to the human spirit's capacity to withstand challenges. Resilience is the silent strength that helps us thrive through adversity and set healthy boundaries. By drawing inspiration from the principles of the Quran and Sunnah, we empower ourselves to confront challenges with determination and grace. In the next chapter, we will explore the concept of power and how to own one's authentic self, utilizing the principles of our faith to empower and uplift women to reach their full potential.

## Points to Ponder & Actions to Take:

- Set your boundaries.
- Communicate your boundaries.
- Shatter that glass ceiling!

# Power – The Ultimate Avatar: Owning Who You Are

---

*"Empowerment is not about being dominant, but about owning your true self, for you are most beautiful when you embrace your authentic soul."*
**– Unknown**

---

True power emanates from embracing one's authentic self, self-awareness, and self-acceptance. The concept of power is undeniably relative, holding different meanings for each of us. However, at its core, power is intricately tied to our identity—the way we perceive ourselves, define ourselves and take ownership of our strengths and weaknesses.

This chapter delves into the essence of authentic power, distinct from external displays, and encourages readers to embrace themselves wholeheartedly. This journey involves self-love, introspection, and contemplation, underpinned by the values of the Quran and Sunnah.

## Defining Our Authentic Power

In Islam, authentic power finds its roots in self-awareness and the recognition of one's identity as a divine creation. In this section, we embark on a journey to distinguish authentic power from mere external influences and delve into what power truly means to us as individuals. While the world often presents us with images of power as dominance or control over others, we seek a deeper understanding rooted in authenticity. Authentic power springs from within, reflecting our true selves and the alignment of our actions with our core values. It's not about overpowering or subduing others but about self-mastery and living in harmony with our beliefs. Drawing inspiration from the Quran and Sunnah, we explore the importance of inner strength, derived from a profound connection with our authentic identity.

As we navigate through this chapter, we will reflect on the teachings of the Prophet Muhammad (peace be upon him) and the guidance found in the Quran. These sacred sources will serve as our compass in the quest for authentic power, shedding light on the timeless principles of self-discovery and living a life aligned with our faith. Ultimately, we will come to recognize that true power emanates from being at peace with our genuine selves and harnessing our inner strengths to navigate life's challenges with grace and conviction.

## Owning Who You Are and Embodying Your Ultimate Avatar

To unlock our authentic power, we must take ownership of our identity and embrace our true selves. Self-acceptance and self-love are integral to this journey. The section draws inspiration from Islamic teachings, emphasizing that self-love should be rooted in gratitude for the divine creation.

Embodying one's ultimate avatar, as guided by Quranic principles and Hadiths, is a profound process of aligning actions with one's true self. It signifies the development of a deep sense of authenticity, self-awareness, and the pursuit of a life in harmony with one's core values. This transformational journey is deeply rooted in Islamic teachings, which provide a strong foundation for self-discovery and personal growth.

1. ***Tawakkul (Trust in Allah):*** The Quran consistently emphasizes the importance of placing trust in Allah (Tawakkul). Trusting in Allah's divine plan and aligning one's actions with faith is central to embodying one's ultimate avatar. This trust enables individuals to take calculated risks, make life changes, and embrace their authentic selves with the knowledge that they are under divine guidance.

2. **Self-Reflection and Accountability:** The Quran encourages self-reflection (Tadabbur) and accountability for one's actions. Reflecting on one's choices, behavior, and values is crucial in aligning with one's true self. This self-awareness allows individuals to make necessary changes to live in accordance with their principles.

3. **Seeking Wisdom (Hikmah):** The Prophet Muhammad (peace be upon him) emphasized seeking wisdom and knowledge. Embarking on the journey of embodying one's ultimate avatar involves continuous learning and acquiring the wisdom necessary to make informed decisions.

4. **Sincerity (Ikhlas):** Sincerity in actions is paramount. The intention behind every action should be aligned with pleasing Allah and not driven by worldly desires. The Quran advises that actions solely for the sake of Allah lead to authenticity.

5. **Taqwa (God-consciousness):** Developing Taqwa, or God-consciousness, is central to the Quranic teachings. It involves being mindful of Allah in all aspects of life. Aligning one's actions with Taqwa means striving to act in ways that are righteous and authentic.

6. **Patience (Sabr) and Gratitude (Shukr):** The Quran teaches the importance of patience and gratitude. Embracing one's true self often involves challenges

and growth. Patience aids in enduring difficulties, while gratitude helps one appreciate their blessings.

7. ***Charity and Compassion:*** Acts of charity and compassion, inspired by Islamic teachings, play a significant role in embodying one's ultimate avatar. Acts of kindness towards others and helping those in need align with core Islamic values.

8. ***Prayer and Supplication:*** Regular prayer (Salat) and supplication (Dua) provide the spiritual foundation for self-discovery and transformation. Connecting with Allah through prayer and seeking guidance is pivotal in the journey of self-realization.

Embodying one's ultimate avatar, as per Quranic principles and Hadiths, is a lifelong journey. It involves continuous self-assessment, self-improvement, and the unwavering pursuit of authenticity. By aligning one's actions with faith-inspired principles, individuals can navigate life's challenges and triumphantly embrace their true selves, fulfilling their purpose in accordance with the divine will. This is a journey that resonates deeply with the core values of Islam and offers a path to spiritual growth and fulfillment.

## The Empowering Impact of Authentic Power

Authentic power transcends the individual, radiating positively into personal relationships, careers, and life's overarching purpose. This section explores how embracing authentic power empowers women to inspire and uplift others. Real-life stories of women during the time of Prophet Muhammad (peace be upon him) demonstrate how embracing their true selves allowed them to radiate the authentic power of women. Their narratives showcase remarkable strength, resilience, and empowerment within the framework of Islamic teachings.

### 1. Khadijah bint Khuwaylid - The Supportive Entrepreneur:

Khadijah (RA), the Prophet's first wife, was a successful businesswoman who supported him during the early years of prophethood. She embodied authentic power by utilizing her strengths as an entrepreneur to provide both financial and emotional stability to the Prophet. Her unwavering belief in him and her financial independence allowed her to play a pivotal role in the early Islamic community.

### 2. Aisha bint Abu Bakr - The Scholar and Educator:

Aisha (RA), one of the Prophet's wives, is renowned for her scholarship, particularly in the fields of Islamic jurisprudence and hadith. She overcame societal norms by actively participating in scholarly debates and teaching, demonstrating how embracing her intellectual power contributed to the development of Islamic jurisprudence.

### 3. *Fatimah bint Muhammad - The Role Model of Piety:*

Fatimah (RA), the daughter of the Prophet Muhammad (PBUH), exemplified piety, humility, and devotion. She embraced her spiritual strength by aligning her life with the principles of Islam. Her dedication to prayer, charity, and compassion towards others highlighted her authentic power as a woman of faith.

### 4. *Nusaybah bint Ka'ab - The Brave Protector:*

Nusaybah, also known as Umm Ammarah, was a courageous companion of the Prophet. She demonstrated her physical and emotional strength on the battlefield, defending the Prophet and his companions during battles. Her unwavering bravery serves as an example of how women harnessed their physical strength to contribute to the early Muslim community.

### 5. *Umm Sulaym - The Empathetic Provider:*

Umm Sulaym was known for her generosity and empathy. She embraced her nurturing power by providing for those in need, particularly during times of hardship. Her acts of kindness, including offering food and support to others, demonstrate the authentic power of compassion and empathy.

These women during the time of Prophet Muhammad are exceptional examples of how embracing their true selves, whether through entrepreneurship, scholarship, piety, bravery, or empathy, allowed them to radiate the authentic power of women. Their stories continue to inspire women today, showing that the power of authenticity and alignment with faith-inspired principles can lead to transformative impact in their communities and the world.

In conclusion, the chapter highlights that authentic power is rooted in self-awareness, self-acceptance, and self-ownership. It encourages us to embark on our journey of embracing and expressing our authentic power by weaving together the threads of purpose, empowerment, and embracing one's divine identity into an inspiring story of their life!

## *Points to Ponder and Actions to Take:*

- Define your authentic power.
- Embody your Ultimate Avatar.
- Live your best life!

# Conclusion

## *Radiant in Your Purpose*

As we come to the end of this transformative journey, let us reflect on the extraordinary voyage we've shared, exploring the depths of womanhood and the divine tapestry that weaves us all together. "Beautiful in God's Eyes: Understanding the Purpose and Power of Women" has been a guiding light, illuminating the path to self-discovery and empowerment.

We've walked through the sacred verses of the Quran and the timeless wisdom of Hadiths, unveiling the profound love and appreciation that the Almighty holds for women. We've peered into the facets of femininity, embracing the inherent strength that comes from self-acceptance. We've ventured into the realms of resilience, independence, and authentic power, realizing that these qualities are not only innate but also nurtured through our choices.

Now, as you close this book and embark on the next chapter of your life, remember that you are a masterpiece of divine design. In your every step, you carry the legacy of countless women who came before you. In your actions, you set an example for generations to follow. In your existence, you hold immeasurable potential.

May you wear your identity with pride and gratitude, may you speak your truth with courage, and may you walk your path with strength and resilience. Your purpose is a shining star, guiding you through life's challenges and triumphs. Aameen!

As you move forward, may you remain radiant in your purpose, unwavering in your power, and, above all, Beautiful in God's Eyes. Aameen! In this truth, you will find the source of your strength and the essence of your existence. For you are not just a part of creation; you are a vital, beautiful, and powerful part of God's eternal masterpiece.

# About The Author

Arjumand is a student and teacher of the Quran. She is an Entrepreneur and A Quranic Guidance Coach on a Mission to Empower Muslim Women to lead their lives according to the Principles of the Quran & Sunnah. Her unwavering commitment to her faith and her multifaceted roles as a daughter, sister, wife, daughter-in-law, and mother underscores her belief in living a purpose-driven life.

Arjumand holds a BA (Hons) in International Business Administration from the UK and an MBA in Finance and E-Commerce from New York, USA. Her academic pursuits are complemented by her extensive religious qualifications, including certified courses in Detailed Tafsir of the Quran, Aqeedah, Dawah Methodologies, 40 Ahadeeth & 110 Hadith Qudsi, Arabic Grammar, Seerah, Blessed Bond, Ashratul Mubasheraat, and Ummahat ul Mumineen.

## About The Author

Arjumand has been teaching the Word-to-Word Translation of the Quran in both English and Urdu since 2008. She was privileged to study under a seasoned Ustadh in Chennai, India, honing her expertise. Her teaching experience also extends to the prestigious Anjuman-E-Himayath E Islam (AHI) Academy in Chennai, India, where she has been studying and instructing since 2004.

With a deep-rooted faith, a profound passion for imparting knowledge, and a wealth of educational and religious qualifications, Arjumand is committed to sharing her insights, wisdom, and experiences through her writing. "Beautiful in God's Eyes - The Purpose and Power of Women" is a testament to her dedication to inspire and empower Muslim Women to embrace their authentic selves and fulfill their God-given potential.

To connect with me, visit my website www.arjumandabdullah.com

www.ingramcontent.com/pod-product-compliance
Lightning Source LLC
LaVergne TN
LVHW041537070526
838199LV00046B/1702